A large ship has reached its destination far out to sea.

The scientists, oceanographers, and other experts aboard are . . .

EXPLORING THE DEEP, DARK SEA

New and Updated

GAIL GIBBONS

Holiday House • New York

TO RANDY MILLER, EXPERT DIVER

Special thanks to Justine Gardner-Smith, news officer;
Dudley Foster, expedition leader of the Alvin *group;*
and Dr. Judith E. McDowell and Susan Wier Mills,
scientists at the Woods Hole Oceanographic Institution,
Woods Hole, Massachusetts.

Copyright © by Gail Gibbons 1999, 2019
First published by Little, Brown and Company in 1999
First Holiday House edition published in 2019
All Rights Reserved
HOLIDAY HOUSE is registered in the U.S. Patent and Trademark Office.
Printed and bound in July 2018 at Toppan Leefung, DongGuan City, China.
www.holidayhouse.com
First Revised Edition
1 3 5 7 9 10 8 6 4 2

Library of Congress Cataloging-in-Publication Data available

ISBN: 978-0-8234-4152-5 (hardcover)

These explorers know that nearly three-fourths of the earth's surface is covered by oceans. And they know that those vast seas can be shallow or as much as 36,000 feet (10,800 meters) deep. The floor of the ocean can be flat for miles, or it can be mountainous. According to this ship's depth finder, the seafloor lies 7,500 feet (2,250 meters) directly below the ship.

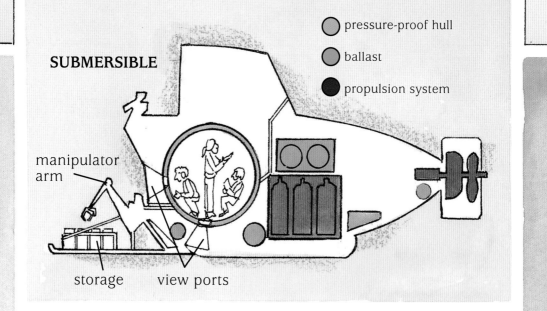

SUBMERSIBLE

pressure-proof hull

ballast

propulsion system

manipulator arm

storage   view ports

The weather is clear and calm, perfect conditions for today's mission. Two oceanographers and a pilot climb into a submersible. This small craft is a diving vessel that can measure, record video, and collect samples of water, plants, and animals found in the ocean. The pilot skillfully maneuvers the submersible wherever the researchers want to go beneath the surface of the ocean.

An **OCEANOGRAPHER** studies the oceans.

Inside, the pilot tests the cameras, life-support systems, underwater lights, mechanical arms, and all other systems. The hatch closes with a gentle thud. It is fastened and secured. "All systems go!" the pilot announces.

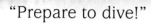

"Prepare to dive!"

The submersible is lifted and moved out over the water, where it is lowered and released. At first it bobs on the sea's surface. Then, as water flows into the ballast tanks, the submersible slowly sinks away from its mother ship in a mass of bubbles.

What an amazing view! Rays of sunlight flash through the warm, blue water. The submersible drops about 100 feet (30.5 meters) per minute. "Two hundred feet…," the pilot says into a microphone, transmitting their depth to the mother ship.

JELLYFISH

HERRING

MACKEREL

THE SUNLIGHT ZONE

The submersible is in the sunlight zone, the area from the water's surface to about 450 feet (150 meters) below. In this shallow part of the ocean, sunlight supports many forms of plant life, both big and small. This is where most marine plants, fish, and other sea creatures live.

PORPOISE

TIGER SHARK

TUNA

A HUMPBACK WHALE is a mammal.

COD

A MAMMAL gives birth to its young. Other creatures lay eggs.

All living things are part of the world's food chain. The oceanic part of the food chain includes the tiniest plants and fish up to the largest marine mammals. Their survival depends on one another. As the submersible continues to sink, with sea creatures darting about, the sea begins to grow darker and colder.

"Four hundred fifty feet . . ."

DOLPHIN

SKATE

THE TWILIGHT ZONE

The small craft now passes into the twilight zone, from 450 feet (150 meters) to 3,300 feet (1,000 meters) down. At first, the water here is a very dark blue. Sunlight fades. It is too dark here for plants to grow. "Look! A squid!" calls out one of the researchers.

JELLYFISH

SQUID

BLACK STAR-EATER

"We're now at fifteen hundred feet. . . ."

The water becomes even darker. The cameras record. The vessel's lights turn on, then off again. Suddenly, quick flashes appear. These twinkling lights are made by the amazing sea creatures living here. They are bioluminescent and can only be seen in the dark.

Many deep-sea creatures create their own BIOLUMINESCENCE with special light organs.

A FLASHLIGHT FISH can be seen from 100 feet (29.9 meters) away.

RED COMB JELLY

The LANTERN FISH has light organs on its head and body.

These creatures of the twilight zone use their bioluminescence to survive. Some send out light patterns to attract mates. Others blind their predators with quick flashes of light. Some camouflage themselves by using light organs on their undersides to blend in with any light flickering from above. As many as four-fifths of all creatures in the oceans are bioluminescent.

The HATCHET FISH uses its light organs for camouflage.

LIGHT FISH

The ANGLERFISH uses a luminous lure to catch food.

BLACK DRAGON FISH

"Approaching thirty-three hundred feet . . ."

It is now pitch-black. The water is much colder. The pilot and the oceanographers are safe because the submersible was designed to withstand the tremendous water pressure surrounding it. Down this deep, the water pressure is as much as a hundred times greater than the air pressure on land.

SLOANE'S VIPER FISH

ARROWWORM

VAMPIRE SQUID

THE DARK ZONE

"It's amazing down here!" the pilot reports. "We're at forty-five hundred feet, and we're recording video." The dark zone lies between 3,300 feet (1,000 meters) and 13,000 feet (3,900 meters) below the water's surface. Some of the creatures moving about look weird and scary. Some are hunters. Others are scavengers, eating what floats down from above.

DRAGON FISH

VIPER FISH

DEEP-SEA ANGLERFISH

SNIPE EEL

As the submersible descends, there are fewer and fewer creatures, only those that have evolved to adapt to their severe surroundings. Food is scarce. Many of the fish have huge jaws and expandable stomachs and often eat prey as big as they are!

GULPER EEL

RED COMB JELLY

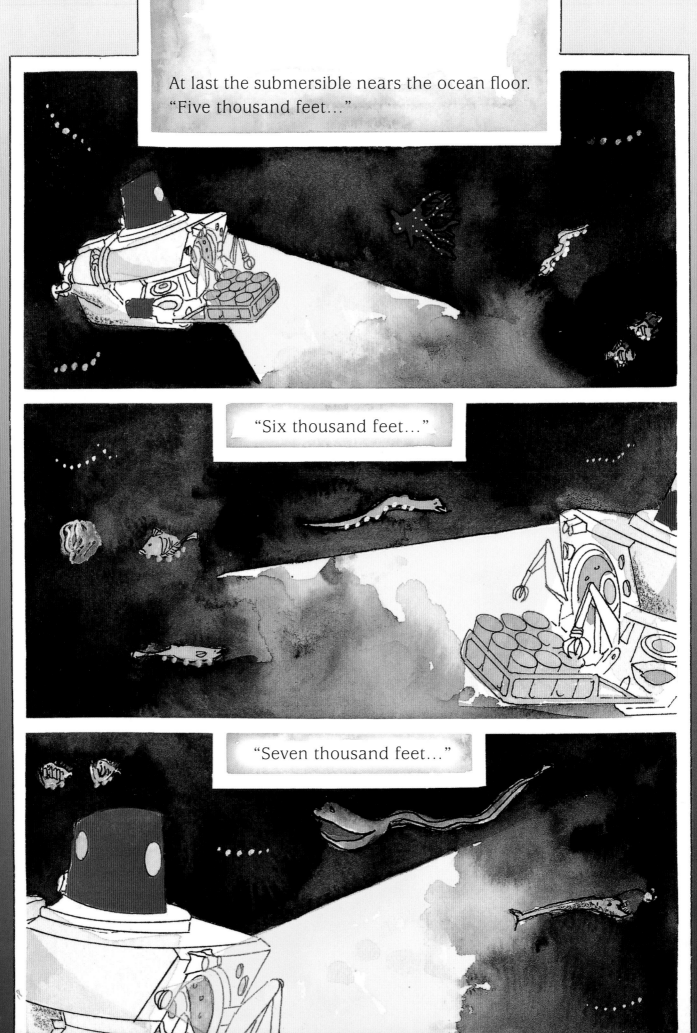

At last the submersible nears the ocean floor. "Five thousand feet…"

"Six thousand feet…"

"Seven thousand feet…"

"We've touched bottom, about seven thousand five hundred feet!"

The pilot guides a mechanical arm to gather samples for study. Lights from the submersible flash on the ocean floor. The water pressure is extremely powerful, two hundred times greater than on the surface.

SNIPE EEL

STARFISH

SEA CUCUMBER

DEEP-SEA ANENOME

The TRIPOD FISH props itself up on long fins. The fins locate food beneath the muddy ocean floor.

BRITTLE STAR

DEEP-SEA CRAB

RATTAIL

The researchers collect specimens until all the sample containers are full. They also take numerous still photos. The video camera continues to run.

BASKET SPONGE

URCHIN

SUN STAR

SEA CUCUMBER

BRITTLE STAR

DEEP-SEA PRAWN

In about four hours the research is complete.
The pilot radios the mother ship that it is time to surface. The submersible steadily makes its ascent. The water changes from black…to dark blue…to light shades of green and blue until…

the submersible breaks through the surface of the smooth ocean waters. A cable is attached to the craft. It is lifted from the sea to the ship's deck. The hatch is opened, and the passengers climb out. Mission accomplished!

Everyone on board the ship gathers around to see what was retrieved from down below. The specimens will be cleaned, identified, and studied in the ship's lab. The photos and video will be viewed. What new discoveries will be made this time?

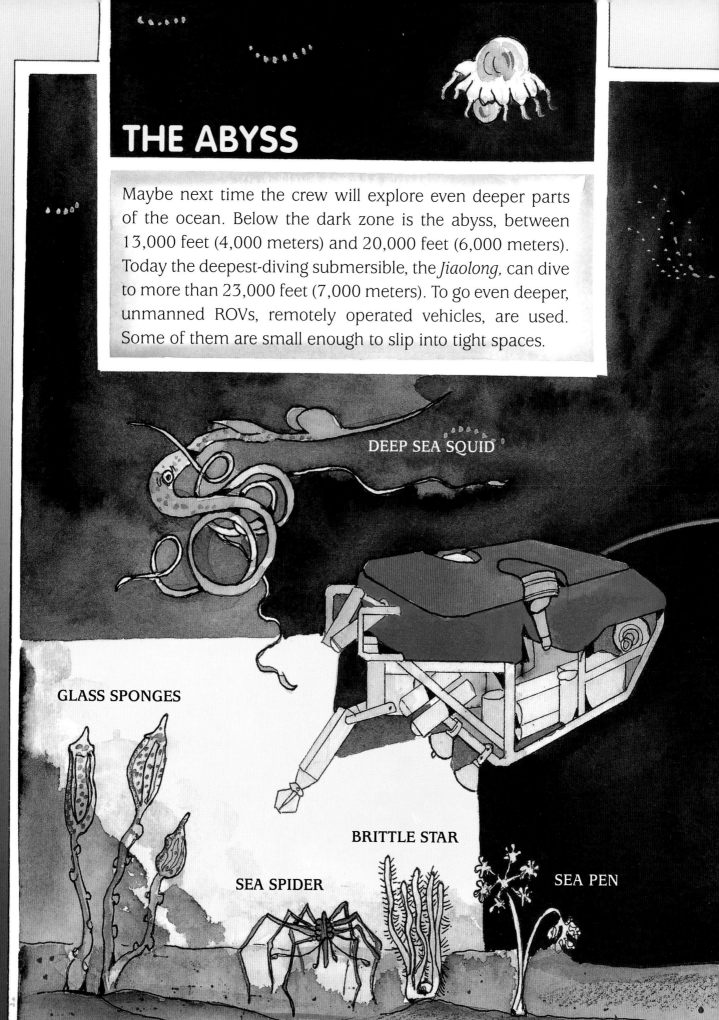

THE ABYSS

Maybe next time the crew will explore even deeper parts of the ocean. Below the dark zone is the abyss, between 13,000 feet (4,000 meters) and 20,000 feet (6,000 meters). Today the deepest-diving submersible, the *Jiaolong,* can dive to more than 23,000 feet (7,000 meters). To go even deeper, unmanned ROVs, remotely operated vehicles, are used. Some of them are small enough to slip into tight spaces.

DEEP SEA SQUID

GLASS SPONGES

BRITTLE STAR

SEA SPIDER

SEA PEN

ROVs are remotely controlled by cable from a submersible or ship. They are equipped with manipulator arms, powerful lights, and cameras that send images directly to the mother ship. The few creatures who live here in the abyss are small, largely because there's not a lot of food.

The ABYSSAL PLAINS cover almost half of the deep sea floor.

RATTAIL

SEA CUCUMBER

DEEP-SEA ANENOME

THE HADAL ZONE

Below the abyss, beginning at 20,000 feet (6,000 meters), is where deep cracks in the ocean floor, called trenches, are found. The Mariana Trench, in the Pacific Ocean, is the deepest part of all the oceans, at 36,000 feet (11,000 meters) deep.

DEEP-SEA ANENOME

POLYCHAETE WORM

Only specifically adapted sea creatures can live in this intense water pressure, where food is scarce, the temperature is icy, and no light penetrates.

DEEP-SEA CUCUMBER

Not long ago, people believed that the deep oceans and the ocean beds were lifeless. How could anything survive in the endless blackness?

BLACK SMOKER CHIMNEY

EELPOUT

WHITE CRAB

GIANT CLAMS

During the 1960s, deep-diving submersibles came into use. They revealed a whole new underwater world. New forms of plant and animal life have been and will be discovered in the deep, dark sea.

TUBE WORMS

SQUAT LOBSTER

DIVING...PAST AND PRESENT

At first

Divers dove without any equipment. They held their breath while gathering sponges, oysters, and other creatures from shallow areas.

1250

The diving bell was invented. Air was trapped in the top of the bell. The diver could breathe until the air supply ran out.

1715

An Englishman, John Lethbridge, used one of the first diving units, a wooden cylinder with a glass view port. He went about 60 feet (18.3 meters) deep.

1930

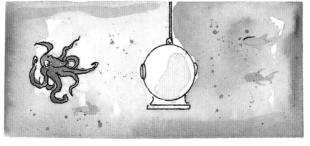

Dr. William Beebe and Otis Barton dove to 1,428 feet (435.3 meters) in a bathysphere, a diving sphere for deep-sea observation, off the coast of Bermuda.

1942

The Aqua-Lung was invented by Jacques-Yves Cousteau and Emile Gagnan. Divers could now stay underwater longer and move freely, because they carried their air supply in a tank on their backs.

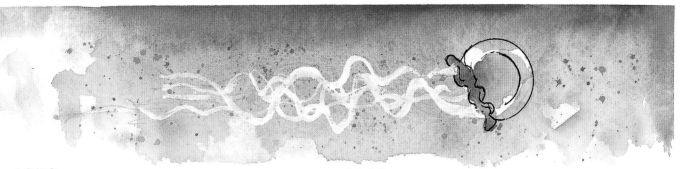

1830

The first diving suit was used. A flexible tube connected the helmet to an air pump on deck.

1892

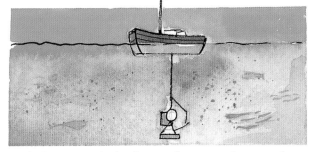

Louis Boutan took the first underwater photographs off the coast of France. He lowered his camera 165 feet (50.3 meters) deep.

1960

Trieste, a bathyscaphe, or deep-diving vessel attached beneath a large cylindrical hull, went to the deepest part of the ocean, the Mariana Trench. It descended 35,000 feet (10,900 meters).

1989

The ROV *Jason Jr.* was launched from *Alvin* to make the historic exploration of the shipwrecked *Titanic.*

The Chinese submersible *Jiaolong* has dived to more than 23,000 feet (7,000 meters). It is the world's deepest diving submersible.

The Present

Vessels like REMUS are exploring the ocean's bottom unmanned. They are used for sea mapping, surveying for hydrothermal vents, locating crashed airplanes, and studying shark behavior.

THE DEEP, DARK SEA

Until about two hundred years ago, many people thought parts of the ocean were bottomless.

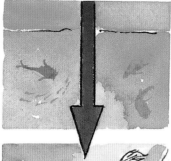

About five hundred years ago, the Italian artist Leonardo da Vinci designed a device for breathing underwater, although he never tried it.

Hydrothermal vents occur where seawater comes in contact with molten rock below the seafloor. Tube worms and giant clams live around some of these vents, where hot water seeps up through the cracks in the ocean floor.

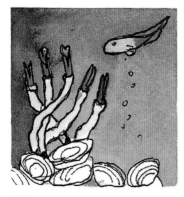

Creatures that live in the deep sea are rarely more than one foot (30 centimeters) long.

At one time, sailors believed that sea monsters lurked in the ocean, waiting to attack.

A giant squid can be up to 43 feet (13 meters) long.

Sometimes minerals in the hot water around thermal vents form large chimneys, which can be as tall as a two-story building. The water rushing out of the chimneys is as black as smoke.

We know less about many parts of the ocean today than we know about the surface of the moon.

Ninety-five percent of the ocean floor is still unexplored.

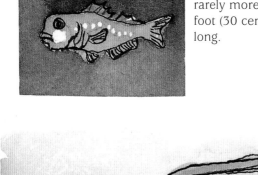